My First Guinea Pig

Veronica Ross

Chrysalis Children's Books

J636.93234

First published in the UK in 2002 by
Chrysalis Children's Books
An imprint of Chrysalis Books Group Plc
The Chrysalis Building, Bramley Road, London W10 6SP

Paperback edition first published in 2004
Copyright © Chrysalis Books Group Plc 2002
Text by Veronica Ross

ISBN 1 84138 399 6 (hb)
ISBN 1 84458 233 7 (pb)

British Library Cataloguing in Publication Data for this book is available from the British Library.

Designer: Helen James
Picture researcher: Terry Forshaw
Consultants: Frazer Swift and Nikki Spevack

Printed in China

10 9 8 7 6 5 4 3 2 1

All photography Warren Photographic/Jane Burton with the exception of:
7 (B), 10 Animal Photography/Sally Anne Thompson;
11 RSPCA Photolibrary/E A Janes; 13 Animal Photography/Sally Anne Thompson;
21 FLPA/Leo Batten.

Contents

Your pet guinea pig

Guinea pigs are great fun to
have as pets, but they do need
to be looked after carefully.
You must feed your pet every day
and give it fresh water to drink.

coat

whiskers

claws

When you go on holiday, you will have to find someone who will look after your guinea pig while you are away.

Young children with pets should always be supervised by an adult. Please see notes for parents on page 32.

What is a guinea pig?

Guinea pigs are small, furry animals with short legs and large front teeth. There are many different kinds of guinea pig. Some have long, silky hair, others have short, tufty hair.

Some guinea pigs have stripes or patches on their fur.

This guinea pig has long hair.

Guinea pigs belong to a group of animals called rodents.

Guinea pigs like to live in a big group.

Newborn guinea pigs

A mother and two newborn guinea pigs.

Newborn guinea pigs are wet and sticky. Their mother licks them clean. The babies are born with all their fur and their eyes are open. They look like small adults. The babies look around, but stay close to their mother.

These three baby guinea pigs are just one week old.

Baby guinea pigs begin to eat solid food after one or two days.

Newborn guinea pigs drink milk from their mother.

Choosing a guinea pig

Choose a guinea pig that looks lively and healthy. Does it seem friendly? If it does, it could be the right one for you.

Ask if you can play with the guinea pigs before you choose one.

These guinea pigs are three weeks old. They will be old enough to leave their mother when they are six weeks.

A guinea pig should have bright eyes, a clean nose and soft, clean-smelling fur.

Guinea pigs can be bought from pet shops, breeders or animal shelters. Your vet may know about breeders and animal shelters where you live.

A place to live

A guinea pig's house is
called a hutch. It should have
a sleeping area with a solid door, and
a part you can see into. Put newspaper
on the floor with wood shavings on top.
Put fresh hay in the sleeping area.

The hutch should be
big enough for your
pet to run around in.

Guinea pigs like a run or an ark in the garden where they can exercise.

Make sure the run can't be knocked over.

The hutch should be waterproof and sheltered from wind and direct sunlight. It should also be raised off the ground. Move it indoors in cold weather.

Settling in

Your guinea pig may be frightened when it first leaves its mother. Leave it to settle in before you pick it up.

Carry your guinea pig home in a special pet carrier like this.

Take your guinea pig to visit a vet as soon as you can. The vet will make sure it is healthy.

Your pet will soon become used to the sound of your voice and will start to feel at home.

Talk to your pet quietly.

Holding your pet

You must always be very gentle with your guinea pig. To pick it up, put one hand under its bottom and the other around its chest. If it struggles put it on the floor.

Stroke your pet before you pick it up.

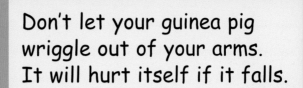

Don't let your guinea pig wriggle out of your arms. It will hurt itself if it falls.

Sit down before you pick up your pet.

When guinea pigs are happy they purr.

Feeding time

Give your guinea pig some
fresh fruit and vegetables every day.
They like cabbage, carrots, celery, broccoli,
apples and pears. Wash the food and cut it
into chunks. Your pet should also have a
bowl of special guinea pig food twice a day.

Fruit and vegetables
will keep your
guinea pig healthy.

Special guinea pig food is made from dried seeds and vegetables.

Buy a special water bottle and attach it to the door of the hutch.

Guinea pigs chew plastic, so make sure the water bottle has a metal spout.

Play time

Your guinea pig
will love being outside in
the garden. Give it some toys
to play with. It will enjoy running
through a plastic pipe or a box
with holes in it.

Guinea pigs like
exploring new toys.

Let's play hide and seek!

Hide some food in a large flower pot and see how long your guinea pig takes to find it!

If you are playing outside don't let your guinea pig out of sight or it might escape!

Keeping clean

It's important to keep your guinea pig's hutch clean. Sweep up droppings and old food every day. Put clean hay in the sleeping area.

Put your pet in a cardboard box while you clean the hutch.

Clean the water bottle at least once a week. Wash the food bowls every day.

Scrub out the hutch once a week with disinfectant from a pet shop. Put in clean newspaper, wood shavings and hay.

Remember to wash your hands when you have finished cleaning.

caring for your pet

Guinea pigs like to have their fur brushed. This is called grooming. Brush your pet gently in the direction the fur grows. Start at the head and brush along the back.

Use a soft brush to groom your pet.

A mineral block will help to keep your pet healthy.

If your pet gets dirty, wash it with warm water and special shampoo from a pet shop.

Guinea pigs use their teeth to pick dirt out of their fur.

Making friends

Guinea pigs like to have lots of friends. Two males or two females from the same litter will get on well.

Guinea pigs like to cuddle up close.

Two male or female guinea pigs who do not know each other may fight.

Rabbits and guinea pigs can be good friends if they are introduced at a young age.

It is not a good idea to keep male and female guinea pigs together because they will have babies. It may be hard to find a home for all the young guinea pigs.

Visiting the vet

Take your pet to the vet for a check-up every year. Your vet will be able to answer any questions you have.

The vet will check your pet's teeth.

Give your guinea pig a block of wood to gnaw. This will stop its teeth from growing too long.

If your pet has little insects in its fur buy some special powder from the vet. This will get rid of the insects.

Cover your pet's face when you use the insect powder.

Words to remember

animal shelter A home for unwanted pets.

ark A large hutch where animals can run around. It is also called a run.

breeder A person who sells animals.

droppings Guinea pig poo.

groom To brush and comb an animal's fur.

hutch The house where a pet guinea pig lives.

litter A group of newborn guinea pigs.

mineral block A special type of food for your guinea pig.

rodent A kind of animal. Rodents have very long teeth. Squirrels and rats are also rodents.

vet An animal doctor.

Index

Notes for parents

If you decide to buy a guinea pig for your child, it will be your responsibility to ensure that the animal is healthy, happy and safe. You will need to make sure that your child handles the guinea pig correctly and does not harm it. Here are some points you should bear in mind before you buy a guinea pig:

• Do you have somewhere to keep a guinea pig?

• A guinea pig costs money to feed. As it gets older, you may have to pay vet's bills as well.

• If you go on holiday, you will need to find someone who can look after your guinea pig while you are away.

• Never keep a guinea pig on its own. Males from the same litter can be kept together as can females. Don't keep males and females together as this will result in unwanted babies.

• Do you have other pets? Cats and dogs usually frighten guinea pigs. Keep them apart.

• Guinea pigs fed on the latest complete diets should not be given mineral supplements unless specifically advised by a vet.

• If you have any questions about looking after your guinea pig, contact your local vet.